Classifying Living Things

Fish

Richard and Louise Spilsbury

Heinemann
LIBRARY

Chicago, Illinois

www.heinemannraintree.com
Visit our website to find out
more information about
Heinemann-Raintree books.

To order:
☎ Phone 888-454-2279
💻 Visit www.heinemannraintree.com
to browse our catalog and order online.

© 2003, 2009 Heinemann Library
an imprint of Capstone Global Library, LLC
Chicago, Illinois

Customer Service: 888-454-2279

Visit our website at www.heinemannraintree.com

Edited by Catherine Clarke and Claire Throp
Designed by Victoria Bevan and AMR Design, Ltd.
Original illustrations © Capstone Global Library, LLC.
Illustrations by David Woodroffe
Picture research by Hannah Taylor

Printed and bound in China by Leo Paper Group

13 12 11 10 09
10 9 8 7 6 5 4 3 2 1

Library of Congress Cataloging-in-Publication Data
Spilsbury, Louise.
    Classifying fish / Louise and Richard Spilsbury.
        p. cm. -- (Classifying living things)
Summary: Explains what fish are and how they differ from
other animals, discussing freshwater fish, sea fish, deep-sea fish,
shallow-water fish, and sharks, among others.
Includes bibliographical references (p.   ) and index.
    ISBN 978-1-4329-2354-9 (lib. bdg. : hardcover) -- ISBN 978-
1-4329-2364-8 (pbk.)
    1. Fishes--Classification--Juvenile literature. 2. Fishes--
Juvenile literature. [1. Fishes.] I. Spilsbury, Richard. II. Title. III.
Series.
    QL618 .S65 2003
    597--dc21
                                    2002015398

Acknowledgments

For Harriet and Miles, rock pool enthusiasts.

We would like to thank the following for permission to
reproduce photographs: Corbis p. 27 (Brandon D. Cole); Digital
Vision p. 29; FLPA pp. 4 (Reinhard Dirscherl), 17 (Minden
Pictures/Matthias Breiter); naturepl pp. 8 (Jeff Rotman), 10
Jurgen Freund), 14 (Juan Manuel Borrero), 18 (Doug Perrine),
19 (Dan Burton), 22 (Doc White), 24 (Jeff Rotman), 25 (Avi
Klapfer & Jeff Rotman); NHPA pp. 23, 26 (Norbert Wu);
Photolibrary pp. 5 (OSF/Zig Leszczynski-AA), 6 (OSF/P. Kent),
9 (OSF/Colin Milkins), 11 (Clover), 12 (Marevision),
13 (OSF/Richard Herrmann), 15 (OSF/Paul Kay), 16 (OSF/
Rodger Jackman), 20 (OSF/Paul Kay), 21 (OSF/Rudie Kuiter);
Science Photo Library p. 28 (Peter Scoones).

Cover photograph of a nurse shark with a school of
juvenile jacks, reproduced with permission of Photolibrary/
OSF/David B. Fleetham.

We would like to thank Ann Fullick for her invaluable
assistance in the preparation of this book, and Martin
Lawrence for his help with the first edition.

Contents

Some words are shown in bold, **like this**. You can find out what they mean by looking in the glossary.

The natural world is full of an incredible variety of **organisms**. They range from tiny bacteria, too small to see, to giant redwood trees over 100 meters (330 feet) tall. With such a bewildering variety of life, it is hard to make sense of the living world. For this reason, scientists classify living things by sorting them into groups.

Classifying the living world

Sorting organisms into groups makes them easier to understand. Scientists try to classify living things in a way that tells you how closely one group is related to another. They look at everything about an organism, from its color and shape to the **genes** inside its **cells**. They even look at **fossils** to give them clues about how living things have changed over time. Then the scientists use all this information to sort the millions of different things into groups.

Scientists do not always agree about the group an organism belongs to, so they collect as much evidence as possible to find its closest relatives.

The whale shark looks like a whale, but it is a fish—it has characteristics in common with all other sorts of fish.

From kingdoms to species

Classification allows us to measure the **biodiversity** of the world. To begin the classification process, scientists divide living things into huge groups called **kingdoms**. For example, plants are in one kingdom, while animals are in another. There is some argument among scientists about how many kingdoms there are—at the moment most agree that there are five! Each kingdom is then divided into smaller groups called **phyla** (singular *phylum*), and the phyla are further divided into **classes**. The next subdivision is into **orders**. Within an order, organisms are grouped into **families** and then into a **genus** (plural *genera*), which contains a number of closely related **species**. A species is a single kind of organism, such as a mouse or a buttercup. Members of a species can **reproduce** and produce fertile offspring together.

Scientific names

Many living things have a common name, but these can cause confusion when the same organism has different names around the world. To avoid problems, scientists give every species a two-part Latin name, which is the same all over the world. The first part of the scientific name tells you the genus the organism belongs to. The second part tells you the exact species. Chub mackerel, for example, has the scientific name *Scomber japonicus*, while the Indian mackerel is *Rastrelliger kanagurta*.

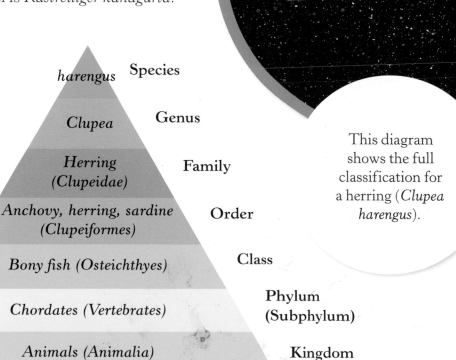

This diagram shows the full classification for a herring (*Clupea harengus*).

harengus	Species
Clupea	Genus
Herring (Clupeidae)	Family
Anchovy, herring, sardine (Clupeiformes)	Order
Bony fish (Osteichthyes)	Class
Chordates (Vertebrates)	Phylum (Subphylum)
Animals (Animalia)	Kingdom

Fish live in water—seawater and fresh water—and have several characteristics that allow us to classify them easily:

- Fish are **vertebrates** (animals with backbones).
- Fish skin is usually covered in protective **scales**.
- Fish get oxygen (a gas dissolved in the water) from the water through special areas of their body called **gills**.
- Most fish use **fins** to swim.
- Fish are ectotherms, which means their bodies are usually the same temperature as the water around them.
- Fish **reproduce** in water, producing soft eggs without shells.

Unless an animal has all these characteristics, it is not a fish. Dolphins, for example, are fish-shaped, live in water, have fins, and are vertebrates, but are not fish because they breathe air, are endothermic (make their own heat), and **suckle** their live-borne young.

Classifying fish

The most important characteristics used in fish classification are the type of bone in their skeleton, type of gill structure, number and shape of fins, and type of scales. Fish are usually sorted into three **classes**: jawless, **cartilaginous**, and bony.

Jawless fish, such as lamprey and hagfish, have no jaws and their skeletons are soft—they are made of **cartilage**, not bone. Jawless fish are thought to be similar to some of the first types of fish that ever lived on Earth.

Lampreys are one of the two classes of jawless fish. Their circular sucking mouth is used to feed on the blood of other animals.

6

Cartilaginous fish have full cartilage skeletons (including jaws), pointed scales, and gills that can be seen through gill slits on either side of their body. This class includes sharks, skates, and rays. There are three **orders** of cartilaginous fish.

Bony fish have skeletons made of bone, flat scales, and gills that are protected by gill covers. More than 90 percent of all fish on Earth are bony fish, including goldfish, cod, and eels. Although there are 49 orders of bony fish, the chart below gives the 15 best known.

This table shows a selection of fish orders.

Fish class	Order	No. of species	Examples
Jawless fish	Lampreys (Petromyzoniformes)	25	lamprey
	Hagfish (Myxiniformes)	20	hagfish
Cartilaginous fish	Sharks (Selachii)	450	great white shark
	Rays and skates (Rajiformes)	350	manta ray
	Ratfish (Chimaeriformes)	25	chimaera
Bony fish	Lungfish (Dipteriformes)	5	African lungfish
	Sturgeons (Acipenseriformes)	25	sturgeon
	Eels (Anguilliformes)	300	freshwater eel
	Herrings (Clupeiformes)	350	anchovy, herring
	Carp (Cypriniformes)	350	minnow, carp
	Salmon (Salmoniformes)	500	trout, pike
	Catfish (Siluriformes)	2,210	wels
	Anglers (Lophiiformes)	150	batfish, goosefish
	Cod (Gadiformes)	450	cod, hake, haddock
	Flying fish (Atheriniformes)	600	flying fish, garfish
	Seahorses (Gasterosteiformes)	150	seahorse, sticklebacks, pipefish
	Scorpionfish (Scorpaeniformes)	700	lionfish, sculpin
	Perch (Perciformes)	7,000	perch, tuna, bass, blennies
	Flatfish (Pleuronectiformes)	500	turbot, plaice, sole
	Boxfish (Tetraodontiformes)	250	sunfish, pufferfish

Some fish look like huge whales or spiky balloons, and others are as flat as pancakes. Many are silver, but others are brightly colored, spotted, or striped. Regardless of how different they look on the outside, on the inside fish have a lot in common.

On the inside

On the inside, every fish has a skeleton, including a backbone. Most fish have hard bones, but the bones of some fish are made of **cartilage**—the same stuff that makes your ears and the tip of your nose hard but flexible.

Bones protect the fish's brain, eyes, and other important **organs** from damage. Some bones do not move, but others do, helped by muscles. For example, muscles open and close a fish's jaw bones.

Do you know ... about fish scales?

Fish skin is usually covered by a protective layer of different shaped transparent **scales**. Scales can be round and smooth on eels, but pointed and rough as sandpaper on sharks.

The trunk fish has scales that fit together like a bony box to protect it.

tail fin

dorsal fins

ventral fin

pelvic fin

pectoral fin

Swimming

Fish have movable **fins** (flaps of skin) that help them move through water. Bones in fins act like the struts in an umbrella to open and close the flap.

Most fins are used to steer, brake, and balance in the water. Many fish have a pair of fins behind their eyes, called the **pectoral** fins. They also have fins on their back, called the **dorsal** fins. Sharks usually have a tall dorsal fin, but other fish, such as eels, have a long, narrow dorsal fin.

The tail fin is used to move through the water. Rows of muscles along the backbone twist the tail from side to side. The tail fin then moves the water behind the fish out of the way while it goes forward. Most fish have tail fins that are symmetrical (have the same top and bottom). Ocean-swimming fish, such as sailfish or flying fish, have crescent-shaped tail fins that help them move faster.

Perch-like fish, such as this freshwater perch, usually have two dorsal fins, and their pectoral fins are positioned halfway up their sides. The **pelvic** fins under their stomach contain one spine.

Do you know ... the best shape for swimming?

Most fish have a smooth, streamlined shape—they are pointed at either end so that water can flow quickly over them. This is often helped by smooth scales and by slime on the skin. Many fish tuck their fins in when they want to move even faster.

All fish have **gills** to breathe with underwater. Amphibians (frogs, toads, and newts) breathe using gills when they are young, but as they grow up they start to breathe with lungs or through their skin. Fish never have lungs— they have gills throughout their lives.

Catching a breath

Gills contain lots of thin blood vessels (tubes). As water moves over the gills, oxygen moves from the water to the blood. The blood then carries the oxygen to parts of the body that need it.

When a fish gulps in water, muscles inside its mouth pump the water across two sets of internal gills and out of its gill slits. Some fish, such as basking sharks, rely on ram breathing. They swim fast with their mouths open, which forces water past their rake-shaped gills. The force traps floating food, such as **plankton**, into their gill rakes. The fish then shake their gills to loosen the trapped food, before sucking it down their throats.

After passing over its gills, water leaves this grouper through two flaps on its sides.

Under pressure

Bony fish swim and float with the help of a **swim bladder**. This is a gas-filled sac (bag) found just below a fish's backbone. The swim bladder acts like a rubber ring to keep a fish **buoyant**.

Cartilaginous fish, such as sharks, have a buoyant oily **liver** instead of a swim bladder. They need to keep swimming most of the time to avoid sinking. Their tail **fins** are usually longer at the top than the bottom, which helps push them up in the water when they move their tails.

Goldfish are often kept as pets. If they are overfed, their swim bladder may stop working and they float on the surface. Many people have disposed of "dead" goldfish, which in fact only needed a change in diet to help them recover!

Do you know ... how fish balance water?

Fish that live in the sea have a problem. The salt in the seawater they take in makes water move out of their body. They have to drink almost all the time to overcome this. However, the body of a freshwater fish contains more salt than the surrounding water, which means water constantly moves into its body. It does not need to drink, but has to urinate almost all of the time to get rid of the water!

Perciformes—an **order** of bony fish—contains over 7,000 different **species**. It gets its name from the perch, a typical member. All have similar anatomy (body construction). The characteristics they have in common include lots of small, sharp teeth and spiny and **cartilaginous** bones in their **fins**.

Variety

There are many distinct groups of perch-like fish, from bass and groupers to mackerel and wrasse. Gobies, blennies, and weevers are generally small fish, often found in shallow seawater or rock pools. They have broad heads, thick lips, and large eyes close together on top of their heads.

Do you know... which is the smallest fish in the world?

The tiniest of all fish is a perch relative. The adult goby, which lives around reefs in the Indian Ocean, is less than 1 centimeter (0.5 inch) long.

Weever fish—hidden danger

- Member of the perch-like group of fish
- Has hard spines in dorsal fins filled with poison
- Spends most of its time buried in sand
- If stung, heat destroys the poison and stops the pain

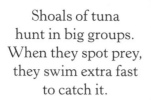

Shoals of tuna hunt in big groups. When they spot prey, they swim extra fast to catch it.

Hunters and hitchers

The biggest perch-like fish are ocean hunters of smaller fish. Tuna, swordfish, and marlin can reach 900 kilograms (2,000 pounds) in weight and grow up to 4.5 meters (15 feet) long. They have special muscles that help them swim faster for longer than most fish. Groups of tuna swim together searching for **shoals** of **prey** such as anchovies. Swordfish and marlin have a long spike on their upper jaw, which they use to stun or injure their prey so that they are easier to catch.

Remoras are a group of unusual perch-like fish. Instead of a **dorsal** fin, they have a special sucker. They use this to hitch a ride on larger sea creatures, saving themselves the effort of swimming. Each species prefers a particular creature to ride on, including whales, sharks, and turtles.

Do you know ... how the Antarctic icefish survives?

The Antarctic icefish is a perch-like fish that can survive in the coldest water on Earth. Its blood does not freeze because it contains chemicals that act like antifreeze in a car radiator.

An easy way of looking at some of the many **orders** of bony fish is by grouping them according to where they live. Several orders of fish almost always live in fresh water.

Carp-like fish

The smallest carp-like fish are brightly colored tetras. The largest is the mahseer, a giant carp that lives in fast-flowing Himalayan rivers. All carp-like fish have **cartilaginous fin** bones, usually low **pectoral** fins, and **pelvic** fins under their stomachs.

Many have special **adaptations** to help them feed. Carp, bream, and goldfish have upper jaws that can extend to suck in food such as insect **larvae** that floats on the water or on the river or lake floor. They grind their food using special throat teeth before swallowing.

Do you know ... how fierce piranhas are?

Red piranhas are small fish with razor-sharp teeth that live in **shoals** in the Amazon River. They have a bad reputation—people think if an animal or person falls into the river, piranhas will tear the flesh off the bones in minutes. In fact, piranhas usually feed on nuts, seeds, or other fish. They rarely attack bigger animals!

Loach are carp relatives that have fingerlike barbels near their mouths. These barbels help them find food, such as worms, living among stones or in mud.

barbels

Did you know ... lungfish can survive out of water?

Most fish die out of water, but the lungfish have **swim bladders** that act like lungs so they can survive dry seasons in parts of Africa and Australia. When the ponds they live in dry up, they bury themselves in mud and curl up in a cocoon (protective covering) of slime, with an airhole to breathe through. They slow down their breathing and can survive many months until rain comes. When the ground is wet enough, they leave their cocoon and slither to the nearest pond, where they can breathe using their **gills**.

All in a name

Catfish have cartilaginous fin bones, **dorsal** fin spines, and broad heads. Catfish usually live in murky or muddy fresh water. They are called catfish because they have lots of **barbels** that look like a cat's whiskers. The barbels act as extra sense **organs** in the murky water.

Bony tongues are mostly **tropical** freshwater fish with large **scales**. They have toothed tongues that bite against rows of teeth on the base of their skull. They include the arapaima—the largest purely freshwater fish, at up to 5 meters (16 feet) long—that has scales tough enough to survive a caiman (freshwater alligator) attack.

Elephant nose fish— a strange feeder

- Large eyes and long "snout"
- Freshwater fish
- Long snout used to suck up food
- Makes electricity, which is used like radar to detect **prey**

Members of several fish **orders** spend part of their lives in fresh water and part in seawater, so they can spawn (lay their eggs) in just the right conditions. They sometimes travel incredibly long distances over regular routes. This is called migration.

Breeding at sea

Eels are snakelike fish, usually without **pectoral** and **pelvic fins**, and with small **scales**. European eels spend most of their adult life living and feeding in European rivers. When they are about 10 years old they migrate up to 6,000 kilometers (3,750 miles) downstream toward the sea, to reach a particular area of the Atlantic coast near the United States. Here they spawn in the deep saltwater and then die.

Their eggs hatch and the large group of baby eels then migrate back to where their parents once lived. Sometimes they even wriggle for hundreds of feet across wet land to reach the right river. Once in the freshwater environment, they grow up fully to become adult eels, and the cycle continues.

Baby eels have transparent skin and are often called glass eels. They migrate in **shoals** of many thousands.

When they migrate, salmon often have to leap up rocky rapids to reach the right area of river. In some spots bears wait to catch a meal.

Breeding in rivers

Salmon, trout, char, and pike all have scale-free heads and no spines in their fins. Pike have a **dorsal** fin near their tails, but salmon have an extra fatty fin behind their dorsal fin.

Salmon spawn in rivers but live in the sea. Adults migrate from food-rich areas of sea to a particular river. They do this using the sun and stars at first, and then by following the taste of river water, which they remember from birth. Male salmon develop humped backs, hook-shaped jaws, and red stripes on their sides to attract females. After spawning, many adults die, exhausted after their long trip. Their eggs hatch into young salmon that live for up to three years in the river before going to sea.

Should we farm fish?

Around the world many **species** of fish, such as salmon and tilapia, are being farmed to provide food for humans. They are reared in artificial containers in rivers or oceans. However, there are concerns about pollution from the waste and disease spreading from farmed fish to wild stock. Farmed fish are also specially bred—if they escape they may interbreed with wild fish and change the species.

Many different **orders** of fish spend their whole lives in shallow seas. Some roam over large areas in **shoals**, while others live on or near the bottom.

Group living

Herring, pilchard, and anchovy are classified together because they have forked tails, flat, silvery bodies, and low **pectoral fins**. They all catch **plankton** to eat using their **gill** rakes (see page 10). Cod, hake, whiting, and pollack are larger fish with two or three **dorsal** fins and small **scales**. **Species** in both of these orders travel in large shoals of up to hundreds of thousands of individuals. All the fish in one shoal hatched from eggs at the same time, so they are all the same age and size.

Being one of many in a big shoal has its advantages. More eyes can spot danger earlier, and groups have ways of protecting one another. If **predators** such as tuna attack a shoal of anchovy, the shoal often bunches together to form a huge, twisting bait ball, sometimes hundreds of feet across. This confuses predators, who cannot easily spot a particular fish to chase, and makes it less likely for each individual fish to be killed.

Thousands and thousands of sardines make a dramatic sight and confuse predators.

On the surface

Flying fish are mostly **tropical** fish that live near the sea's surface. They have large pectoral (and sometimes also **pelvic**) fins positioned high on their bodies. These winglike fins help them to glide or skip above water to get extra speed to escape predators.

Ocean sunfish are massive, slow-swimming fish, up to 4 meters (13 feet) across, with no tail fin and long fins at the top and bottom. They have four teeth that form a beak to catch slippery food such as jellyfish. Their smaller relatives, pufferfish and porcupine fish, can puff up their spiky bodies with water to look bigger if a predator approaches.

On the bottom

When flatfish such as plaice, turbot, sole, and flounder are babies, they have an eye on each side of their heads. As they develop, one eye moves so that they are both on the top side of the fish. They spend much of their time lying flat on one side on the bottom of the sea. Having eyes on top allows them to spot a passing meal, such as shrimp, and approaching danger.

Dabs—invisible fish?
- Flatfish
- Both eyes on top surface
- **Camouflaged** skin
- Burrows into sand to hide from **prey**

19

Nearly 30 percent of the world's fish **species** live in shallow waters near coasts and reefs. Tiny coral animals build rocklike reefs in shallow, warm, **tropical** seawater. Many **orders** of fish live around reefs because there are lots of **prey** to catch and places to hide from danger.

Squirrelfish are reef fish with large eyes and protruding lower jaws that make their faces look a bit like squirrels. Many live in crevices in reefs and come out to feed mostly at night. Their faded red color is difficult to see in the dark water, so they can hunt smaller fish more easily without being spotted.

Scorpionfish, stonefish, and gurnards have large heads with bony ridges under their eyes, used as armor, and strong spines on their **dorsal fins**. Scorpionfish often have poison-filled spines for further protection from **predators**. They are brightly striped to warn other animals to avoid their sting. Stonefish are masters of disguise. They lie half-buried in sand, their spiny bodies cloaked with seaweed, waiting to ambush prey.

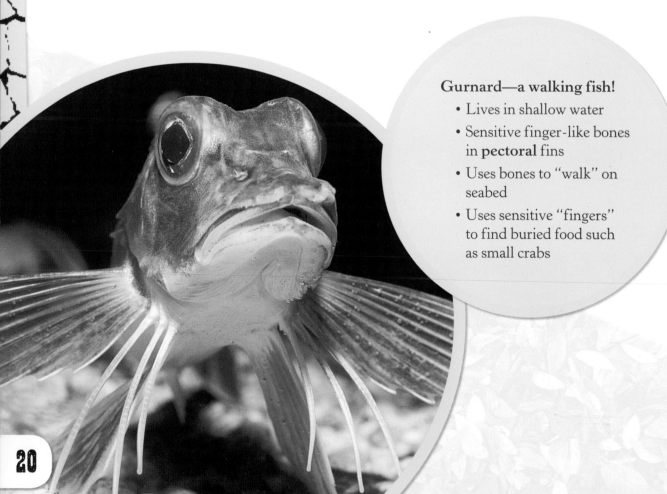

Gurnard—a walking fish!

- Lives in shallow water
- Sensitive finger-like bones in **pectoral** fins
- Uses bones to "walk" on seabed
- Uses sensitive "fingers" to find buried food such as small crabs

Seahorses, pipefish, and sticklebacks

Fish such as seahorses, pipefish, and sticklebacks have ridged, armored bodies with no **scales**. They have tube-shaped heads and mostly small fins. Some sticklebacks live in shallow seawater. The 15-spined stickleback got its name because of the 15 short, sharp spines in front of its dorsal fin. The male builds a small nest out of seaweed for the female to lay her eggs in.

Pipefish and seahorses swim weakly, mainly using their dorsal fin. Pipefish are shaped like long pipes, and seahorses have an angled, horse-shaped head. Seahorses coil their tail around seaweed to hold on if the water is moving or if they want to rest. A female lays her eggs in a special pouch on the male's stomach. Then the male cares for the eggs until they hatch.

Some seahorses, such as the pygmy seahorse of Indonesia, are brightly colored for **camouflage** among bright coral. Others, such as the sea dragon, are covered in ragged skin to make them look like floating seaweed.

When baby seahorses have hatched from their eggs, they leave the safety of their father's pouch.

Life in the deepest oceans is very demanding. The weight of all the water above means that there is great **water pressure** in the deeper parts of the sea. At several miles below the surface, water is very cold and almost completely dark. Deep-sea fish need special **adaptations** to be able to live there, such as large eyes to sense any light so far from the surface.

Seeing the light

Many deep-sea fish make their own light using special chemicals. Lantern fish have rows of lights on their sides that flash on and off. These act as a signal to other lantern fish, so that they can remain close together. The lights also attract their **prey**, such as shrimp and small fish, which they catch in shallower waters at night.

Anglerfish have loose, scaleless skin, large heads, and mouths with sharp teeth. They have a long **dorsal fin** bone with a dangling blob of skin at the end that produces light. The fish folds this forward like a fishing rod and uses the light as bait to attract prey toward its mouth.

The Atlantic football fish has a ball-shaped head. Its "rod" is folded back as it swims.

Grabbing a meal

There is such a shortage of food in the depths that fish living there have to be certain of catching any meal that is going by. Several **orders** of fish spend most of their time on the bottom searching for food. Spiny eels have bony heads, long, tapering bodies, and **larvae** a bit like those of shallow water eels. They swim head-down along the bottom until they find starfish to eat.

Hatchetfish are shaped like a small ax. They have big, upturned mouths and large eyes to see and catch food moving toward them from the lighter waters above. Their relatives, viperfish and dragon fish, have fangs that are so long they cannot close their mouths. Both these fish attract prey by making light and then swimming fast to spear their meal before swallowing it. Dragon fish make a special red light to spot their prey. The prey cannot see this light, so the dragon fish can sneak up on them.

Deep sea gulper eel—surviving in the depths

- Lives at great depths
- Can grow up to 2 m (6.5 ft) long
- Very large jaws—can swallow prey bigger than itself because does not know where next meal will come from

Sharks range from 10-meter- (35-feet-)long whale sharks weighing 20 tons down to small dogfish. They have some of the most notorious jaws in the oceans, but they are not made of bone. Sharks are one of three **orders** of **cartilaginous** fish.

Bone and skin

Shark skin is covered in pointed **scales**. The scales interlock much like chainmail armor to protect sharks from damage and to make them streamlined. Sharks have five or seven **gill** slits on each side of their body, unlike bony fish, which only have one on each side. Their jaw is loosely connected to their skull, which means they can stretch their mouths forward to bite. Their **fins** are fleshy, and typically their tail fins are longer on top.

A headstart

Unlike most fish, the eggs of some shark **species** hatch inside, and these species give birth to live young. Others, such as the bullhead shark, lay their delicate eggs in protective capsules, often called mermaids' purses. These purses are split open and discarded by the young once the eggs hatch.

This great white shark, like all sharks, remains **buoyant** because its massive **liver**—up to a quarter of its body weight—is full of lightweight oils.

Shark teeth

Shark teeth grow in two or three rows. Rows of new, sharp teeth move forward out of the jaw—kind of like a tooth conveyor belt—to replace any worn or broken ones at the front. The teeth vary in shape and size. Sharks like the sandtiger have slender and hook-shaped teeth to catch fish. Smoothhounds have blunt teeth for crushing **prey** such as crabs. Those like the great white shark have triangular and dagger-shaped teeth to cut the flesh of larger prey. Several sharks, such as basking and whale sharks, have tiny teeth. They feed on the **plankton** they catch using their gill rakes (see page 10).

Feeding habits

Sharks vary widely in the way they catch prey. The megamouth swims with its massive mouth open, feeding on deep-sea plankton. The great white shark is a fast-swimming **predator** of large fish and sea mammals such as whales. The sawfish has a long, flat snout with large, toothlike scales along the sides—it looks a little like a chainsaw—that it slashes through **shoals** of fish.

Hammerhead shark—
a unique head shape
- Underwater predator
- Head shaped like a hammer head with eyes at each end
- Head shape linked to method of sensing hidden prey. It works a bit like a metal detector.

Did you know ... some sharks are endangered?

Sharks are famous for killing swimmers, but in fact there are millions of sharks and very few human casualties. In fact, it is sharks that are at risk. Thanks to human activities, from hunting to pollution, a number of shark species are **endangered**, and some have become **extinct**.

Rays and skates are close relatives of sharks. They are grouped separately from sharks because they have flattened bodies with eyes on top and spend much of their time lying on the seafloor. They swim by flapping their wide **pectoral fins** like wings.

Unlike flatfish, their **gill** slits and mouth are underneath. Since their mouths are flat against the ground, they have holes behind their eyes where they suck in water to flow over the gills inside.

Skates and rays usually have a whiplike tail and often have spiny skin. The skin on top is commonly patterned to look like the seafloor or to change the shape of their outline. This **camouflage** helps them hide from **predators**, but it also helps them catch their own **prey**. They often lie partly buried in sand and flop over prey, such as flatfish, crabs, and clams, to catch them.

Stingray—lethal dart
- Around 1 m (3.3 ft) across
- Mouth and gill slits on underside
- Long, sharp spine above tail
- Spine contains poison for defense if attacked or stepped on

pectoral fin

gill slits

pectoral fin

mouth

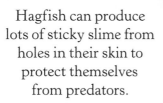

Hagfish can produce lots of sticky slime from holes in their skin to protect themselves from predators.

Big brother

Rays and skates are usually up to 1 meter (3.3 feet) across. The manta ray is an exception—it can reach 9 meters (30 feet) across and weigh a ton. It feeds on areas of **plankton** or small fish in **tropical** waters. Manta rays swim in slow somersaults through their food source and use the large flaps in front of their eyes as paddles to funnel plankton into their open mouths.

Jawless fish

One **class** of fish does not have jaws. These strange fish include two groups: the lampreys and the hagfish. These fish have small **cartilaginous** skeletons, no **scales**, and eel-like bodies. Without jaws to open and close their mouth, they have to suck in their food from other fish. Lampreys attach themselves to other fish by using their mouths. Circles of teeth scrape the skin of their carrier and they suck in the blood. Hagfish have sharp spikes on their tongues to grate bits of flesh off dead or dying animals, even fish caught in nets. They are blind and find food using their sense of smell and their **barbels**.

Do you know ... what a ratfish is?

Ratfish are cartilaginous fish with no scales and with gill covers. They got their name because of their long, pointed tails and pointed snouts.

The number of different types of living **organisms** in the world is often called **biodiversity**. Sadly, all over the world, **species** of living organisms are becoming **extinct**. This means that these organisms no longer exist on Earth. There are many different reasons for this. Extinction has always happened—some species die out and other species **evolve**. But today people are changing the world in ways that affect all other species.

People are damaging rivers, lakes, oceans, and seas. We are polluting the air and the water. We have overfished the oceans, driving many species to the verge of extinction. Our use of fossil fuels, such as oil and gas, is causing global warming. Global warming is a rise in Earth's average temperature and a change in weather patterns. When the temperature and the weather change, it can have a serious effect on living things, including fish.

The coelacanth—a living fossil?

Until recently, people knew the coelacanth as a **fossil** fish that had been extinct for thousands of years. Then, in 2007, a fisherman caught one, and by chance a visiting scientist recognized what it was. Since then several have been caught and studied. However, the coelacanth and thousands of other species of fish now face extinction for certain.

The ocean is still largely a mystery, so many fish species could be extinct before we even know they exist!

Coral reefs are described as the rain forests of the sea—they have a huge range of species of fish living in and around them. However, pollution and global warming are leading to the death of huge areas of coral, and when the coral dies, so do the fish associated with it.

What can be done?

To help prevent more fish from becoming extinct, people need to take care of the seas, oceans, and fresh water of Earth, protecting the places where fish live and controlling levels of fishing. If we can do this, many species will be saved. Biodiversity is important—we need as many species of fish as possible for the future.

The human threat to coral reefs also threatens many different species of fish and other living things.

Glossary

adaptation special feature, such as fins, that helps living things to survive in their particular habitat

barbel fleshy, sensitive whisker

biodiversity different types of organisms around the world

buoyant able to float

camouflage color, shape, or pattern that helps an animal hide in its environment

cartilage firm but flexible skeleton material

cartilaginous having cartilage rather than bone

cell smallest unit of life

class classification grouping. There are three classes of fish, each containing several orders.

dorsal in or attached to the back

endangered when an animal or plant species is in danger of becoming extinct (dying out)

evolve change over time

extinct when a species has died out and no longer exists

family classification grouping. Herrings are a family of bony fish.

fin flap of skin that helps a fish swim

fossil remains of an organism that once lived on Earth

gene structure by which all living things pass on characteristics to the next generation

genus (plural **genera**) classification grouping. In each family of fish, there are usually several genera.

gill structure used for breathing underwater

kingdom in classification, the largest grouping of living things (for example, animals)

larvae young hatched from an egg

liver body organ that cleans the blood

order classification grouping. There are three orders within the class of cartilaginous fish.

organ part of the body with a specific job to do, such as the liver or heart

organism living thing

pectoral in or attached to the chest bones

pelvic in or attached to the hip bones

phylum (plural **phyla**) classification grouping. Each phylum is divided into different classes.

plankton tiny animals and plants that float in water

predator animal that hunts and eats other animals

prey animal that is hunted and eaten by another animal

reproduce give birth to babies

scales overlapping or interlocking pieces that form a protective layer over fish skin

shoal group of fish

species classification grouping. A species is a particular type of organism, such as a turbot.

suckle feed young at the breast

swim bladder gas-filled sac (bag) inside bony fish that helps keep them buoyant

tropical found in the Tropics (near the equator, where it is warmest)

vertebrate animal with an internal backbone

water pressure weight of water pushing against an organism's body

Books

Pyers, Greg. *Classifying Animals: Why Am I a Fish?* Chicago:
Raintree, 2006.

Snedden, Robert. *Living Things: Fish.* Mankato, Minn.:
Smart Apple Media, 2009.

Stefoff, Rebecca. *Family Trees: The Fish Classes.* Tarrytown, N.Y.:
Marshall Cavendish, 2007.

Websites

www.mnh.si.edu
This is the website of the National Museum of Natural History in
Washington, D.C.

www.fishid.com/facts.htm
You can find some interesting fish facts on this web page.

www.nationalaquarium.com
This is the website of the National Aquarium in Washington, D.C., which
is a great place to visit.

http://kids.yahoo.com/animals/fishes
On this web page there are lots of links to information about individual fish.

www.endangeredspeciesinternational.org/fish.html
This web page uses some difficult words, but it provides a lot of information
about endangered fish.

Index